Preparatory Level

Specific Skill Series

Identifying Inferences

William H. Wittenberg

Fifth Edition

SRA/McGraw-Hill
Columbus, Ohio

Cover, Back Cover, John Downer/Masterfile

SRA/McGraw-Hill

A Division of The **McGraw·Hill** *Companies*

Send all inquiries to:
    SRA/McGraw-Hill
    8787 Orion Place
    Columbus, OH 43240-4027

ISBN 0-02-688000-8

  5 6 7 IPC 02 01

To the Teacher

PURPOSE:

IDENTIFYING INFERENCES is designed to develop one of the most difficult interpretive skills—arriving at a *probable* conclusion from a limited amount of information. IDENTIFYING INFERENCES requires the readers to *read between the lines*. They must utilize previously acquired knowledge and past experiences in order to fully comprehend the message of the text.

FOR WHOM:

The skill of IDENTIFYING INFERENCES is developed through a series of books spanning ten levels (Picture, Preparatory, A, B, C, D, E, F, G, H). The Picture Level is for pupils who have not acquired a basic sight vocabulary. The Preparatory Level is for pupils who have a basic sight vocabulary but are not yet ready for the first-grade-level book. Books A through H are appropriate for pupils who can read on levels one through eight, respectively. **The use of the *Specific Skill Series Placement Test* is recommended to determine the appropriate level.**

THE NEW EDITION:

The fifth edition of the *Specific Skill Series* maintains the quality and focus that has distinguished this program for more than 25 years. A key element central to the program's success has been the unique nature of the reading selections. Nonfiction pieces about current topics have been designed to stimulate the interest of students, motivating them to use the comprehension strategies they have learned to further their reading. To keep this important aspect of the program intact, a percentage of the reading selections have been replaced in order to ensure the continued relevance of the subject material.

In addition, a significant percentage of the artwork in the program has been replaced to give the books a contemporary look. The cover photographs are designed to appeal to readers of all ages.

SESSIONS:

Short practice sessions are the most effective. It is desirable to have a practice session every day or every other day, using a few units each session.

SCORING:

Pupils should record their answers on the reproducible worksheets. The worksheets make scoring easier and provide uniform records of the pupils' work. Using worksheets also avoids consuming the exercise books.

To the Teacher

It is important for pupils to know how well they are doing. For this reason, units should be scored as soon as they have been completed. Then a discussion can be held in which pupils justify their choices. (The Integrated Language Activities, many of which are open-ended, do not lend themselves to an objective score; thus there are no answer keys for these pages.)

GENERAL INFORMATION ON *IDENTIFYING INFERENCES:*

The difference between a *conclusion* and an *inference*, as presented in this series, is that a conclusion is a logical deduction based upon conclusive evidence, while an inference is an "educated guess" based upon evidence that is less than conclusive. Read this sample:

> Captain Fujihara quickly parked the fire truck, grabbed his helmet, and rushed into the house at 615 Oak Street.

You can *conclude* that Captain Fujihara knows how to drive because that ability was required to park the fire truck. You can *infer* that there is a fire at 615 Oak Street because Captain Fujihara took his helmet and rushed into that house. This is an inference because firefighters do rush to put out fires. It is an inference because there may be another reason for the firefighter's rushing to the house. Captain Fujihara may live there and be late for supper. Thus an inference is supported by evidence, but the evidence is not necessarily conclusive.

SUGGESTED STEPS:

1. Pupils read the text. On levels C–H, after reading, pupils examine the statements that follow the text to determine whether each is a factually true statement (T), a false statement (F), or a valid inference (I). ("True" statements are those about which the reader can be *certain* from the text.) On lower levels, pupils determine which statement about the text or picture is probably true.
2. Then pupils reexamine the text or picture for evidence to support their decisions.
3. Pupils record their answers on the worksheets.

RELATED MATERIALS:

Specific Skill Series Placement Tests, which enable the teacher to place pupils at their appropriate levels in each skill, are available for the Elementary (Pre-1–6) and Midway (4–8) grade levels.

In a story, a writer does not tell you everything. You have to think about what the writer *does* tell you. Then you can make guesses about things that are probably true. Think about this story:

> Len went over to the sink. He filled a tall glass with water.

The writer does not say that Len was thirsty. But you can guess that he was. How do you know this? You know from clues in the story. You know from what you yourself have seen and done.

When you make a guess like this, you are making an **inference**. An inference is a guess you make from the things the writer tells *plus* what you know.

In this book, you will look at a picture and read a story. Think about what the story tells. Think about what else is probably true. Then read the two sentences under the story. One sentence will not be true. The other sentence will be a guess that can be made about the story. It will say something that is *probably* true. Choose the sentence that is probably true.

Mary has fun after school. She takes a book and goes to the park. You can see her sitting under the same tree every day.

Which is probably true?

(A) **The park is open at night.**

(B) **Mary likes to read.**

"Today we will go to the zoo," said Father. "Where do you want to go next?" Bob said he wanted to go to a farm.

Which is probably true?

(A) **Father will stay home.**

(B) **Bob likes animals.**

Tammy saw the trucks go by. She ran to see the fire. Soon the fire was out. The trucks drove away. Tammy went back to her house.

Which is probably true?

(A) The trucks were fire trucks.

(B) Tammy's house was on fire.

Monica wanted a new game that she had seen on TV. Mother told her to wait. Mother said, "Your birthday will be here soon."

Which is probably true?

(A) **Monica will never get the new game.**

(B) **Monica will get the game on her birthday.**

Tom ran into the house. He took off his hat and coat. They were all wet. Tom was happy to be in the house.

Which is probably true?

    (A) It was raining out.

    (B) Tom had a new hat and coat.

Ann wanted to ride her bike to the store. But she didn't have her bike. "Maybe Jim will be back soon," said Ann.

Which is probably true?

(A) Ann has two bikes.

(B) Jim has Ann's bike.

Betty got a book about making boats. The next day she began to make one. After ten days, Betty went fishing in her boat.

Which is probably true?

(A) **Betty can read.**

(B) **The boat was painted red.**

Bob looked at the lions. He was surprised that they were so big. Bob was happy the lions were in the zoo.

Which is probably true?

(A) **Bob wanted a lion for a pet.**
(B) **Bob had never seen a lion before.**

"Look at what I made!" said Eric. He ran to get his friends. He wanted to show them what he had made.

Which is probably true?

(A) **Eric's friends are sleeping.**

(B) **Eric likes what he made.**

Ann put on an old hat. Mary looked at Ann. She began to laugh. Then Bob saw Ann. Bob began to laugh, too.

Which is probably true?

(A) **The hat made Ann look funny.**

(B) **Bob did not know it was Ann.**

Erica went up the tree. She could see far away. She could see her cat playing in the park. Erica liked sitting in the tree.

Which is probably true?

(A) It was a tall tree.

(B) Erica didn't have a pet.

Jill called Ben. Ben didn't come. He was in back of a big tree. "Where is Ben?" said Jill. "He said he wanted to play a game!"

Which is probably true?

(A) Ben doesn't like games.

(B) Ben is hiding.

A. Exercising Your Skill

Look at the picture of Bob at the zoo. Then read the list below. Three of the words belong in the list. One word does not belong. Write the heading on your paper. Then write the words that belong under the heading.

How Bob Felt

thrilled
bored
interested
excited

B. Expanding Your Skill

Talk about the picture.

- What is happening in the picture?
- How do you think Bob feels? How can you tell?
- How might the lions scare Bob?
- What could Bob do?

C. Exploring Language

Draw a picture of your favorite animal at the zoo. Give your drawing a name. Write the name on your drawing. Then copy the story below to tell about your trip to the zoo. Use your own words to fill in the blanks.

My Trip to the Zoo

I love the zoo! My favorite animal is the ____ . I like it because it looks ____ . Then I watch the ____ . I also like to see the baby ____ play.

D. Expressing Yourself

Pretend you are a reporter at the zoo. Ask these animals what they like best about life at the zoo.

giraffe   skunk   tiger   monkey

Do one of these things.

1. Report to your classmates about what each animal said.
2. Draw a picture of each animal at home in the zoo.
3. Ask your classmates to draw a picture of their favorite animal.

"Your dog eats too much," said Tom. "I can tell by looking at it. You should not give it so much food."

Which is probably true?

(A) **The dog is fat.**

(B) **Tom has a pet.**

It was a hot day. Betty went out of her house. She sat on the grass for a long time. Betty said, "This is fun."

Which is probably true?

(A) **Betty does not like her house.**

(B) **Betty likes the sun.**

"Where is my book?" said Ann. "I can't find it." Ann looked and looked. But she could not find her lost book.

Which is probably true?

(A) **Ann never had a book.**

(B) **Ann wanted her book.**

Bob looked down. He could see his house and the school. He could see all of the city. "I want to fly in an airplane again," said Bob.

Which is probably true?

(A) **Bob didn't fly high.**

(B) **Bob liked the ride.**

"I'm going to help Mother take out the old papers," said Mary. "She needs help."

"Wait," said Betty. "I'll go with you."

Which is probably true?

(A) **Betty will help, too.**

(B) **Mother is not at home.**

Jim found a toy in the park. He was going to take it home. But then he saw a little boy crying. Jim went over to the boy.

Which is probably true?

(A) **Jim laughed at the boy.**

(B) **Jim gave the toy to the boy.**

"Where is my cat?" asked Ann. "It was in the house." Then Ann saw that the back door was open. Ann said, "Now I know where my cat is."

Which is probably true?

(A) The cat went out of the house.

(B) The cat is hiding in the house.

Father went to work. When he came home, the grass was cut. "Thank you, Rosa," said Father. "I didn't have time to cut the grass."

Which is probably true?

(A) **Rosa cut the grass.**

(B) **Father was not happy.**

Tom was at a farm. A pig began to go after Tom. Tom ran to a tree and went up it. He was happy the tree was there.

Which is probably true?

(A) **Tom liked the pig.**

(B) **Tom got to the tree first.**

"After this game, let's go out and play with our friends in the park," said Jim.

"That will be fun," said Ann. "But let's ride our bikes to the park."

Which is probably true?

(A) The park is far away.

(B) It's hot out.

A bird sat in a tree. Mary put some bird food on the grass. The bird came out of the tree. It began to eat the bird food.

Which is probably true?

(A) The bird could not fly.

(B) Mary liked the bird.

"Wait for me after school," said Tom. "I'll walk home with you." Rosa said she would wait for Tom. But after school Tom could not find Rosa.

Which is probably true?

(A) Tom rode his bike home.

(B) Rosa forgot to wait for Tom.

A. Exercising Your Skill

Look at the picture. Mary and Betty are going to help Mary's mother take out old papers. How do you think they feel? Read the lists. In each list two of the words belong. One word does not belong. Write the headings on your paper. Then write the words that belong under each heading.

How Mother Feels	How Mary and Betty Feel
pleased	selfish
angry	helpful
grateful	kind

B. Expanding Your Skill

Household chores can be fun. Below are three lists of jobs done around the house. Put each heading at the top of the right list. Add one more job to each list.

Kitchen Chores	Bedroom Chores	Pet Chores
make bed	bathe the pet	wash dishes
put away clothes	feed the pet	prepare meals
clean up toys	walk the pet	set table

C. Exploring Language

Draw a picture of yourself doing your favorite household job. Give the picture a title. Then copy the story that follows on your paper. Use your own words to fill in the blanks.

My Chores

I have some jobs to do at my house. First, I help clean ____ . Then I put away my ____ . At meals, I might set the ____ . I might also clear the ____ . Helping around the house is fun!

D. Expressing Yourself

Do one of these things.

1. With two friends, pretend you are Mary, Betty, and Mary's mother. Act out what they might do and say while they are cleaning out the old papers.

2. Pretend you are a reporter from your school paper. Ask Mary, Betty, and Mary's mother questions like these:

   What job did you each do?

   How did you each feel when you were finished?

Jim gave Ann a game. Betty gave her a book. Then they all had cake to eat. The children had fun at the party.

Which is probably true?

(A) **It was Ann's birthday.**

(B) **Jim made the cake.**

"I want my boat to look good," said Mary. She put her boat in back of her house. Then Mary began to paint the boat.

Which is probably true?

(A) **Mary ran out of paint.**

(B) **The boat didn't look new.**

Bob was riding his bike down a hill. A wagon was in the road. Bob saw the wagon, but he could not stop in time. Bob hit the wagon.

Which is probably true?

(A) **Bob was riding fast.**

(B) **Bob liked the ride.**

Christina went to the store. She got apples and food for her dog. When Christina got home, she said, "Oh! I forgot to get fish food."

Which is probably true?

(A) **Christina has pet fish.**

(B) **Christina does not like animals.**

The baby cries when it's wet. It cries when it wants food. Its father and mother need to look to see if the baby is wet or wants food.

Which is probably true?

(A) The baby never cries.

(B) The baby can't talk.

Andy looked in the toy box. He looked under the bed. "I wish I could find that ball!" he said.

Which is probably true?

    (A) Andy wants to play ball.
    (B) Andy is tired.

A man was cutting down a tree. Kayla was by the tree. Kayla ran away. She didn't want to get hit.

Which is probably true?

(A) **The tree hit Kayla.**

(B) **Kayla saw the tree falling.**

"I'll see you after school," said Ann. "We can play ball in the park."

"That will be fun," said Juan. "Then we can play a game at my house."

Which is probably true?

(A) **Juan does not like Ann.**

(B) **Ann and Juan are friends.**

Jim read two stories. One story was about a horse and a cow. The other story was about a car. Jim liked the story about the horse and the cow.

Which is probably true?

(A) **Jim likes animals.**

(B) **Jim can't read well.**

Mary didn't like her bike. It looked old. Mary went to the store. She came back with a can of paint. "Soon my bike will look new," said Mary.

Which is probably true?

(A) **Mary likes to walk.**

(B) **Mary is going to paint her bike.**

Father took his dog for a walk. When they got by the lake, the dog wanted to run. It wanted to run into the lake.

Which is probably true?

(A) Father went for a swim.

(B) The dog likes to play in water.

Bob was playing with his airplane. The airplane went high. It went into a big tree. Bob could not get the airplane. He ran home to get Father.

Which is probably true?

(A) Father can get the airplane.

(B) The airplane didn't fly.

Rosa got a fish. She put the fish on a step and went into her house. Rosa's cat saw the fish. When Rosa came out, the fish was not there.

Which is probably true?

(A) **Rosa ate the fish.**

(B) **The cat took the fish.**

Ann put her coat on the grass. A dog came and took the coat. The dog ran away. Ann ran after the dog.

Which is probably true?

(A) Ann wanted her coat.

(B) Ann didn't like her coat.

A. Exercising Your Skill

Look at the picture below. Rosa has just returned from a fishing trip. Think about places to fish and what you need to bring. Then complete the lists next to the picture. Write on your paper.

Places to Fish

_____
_____
_____

Fishing Things I Need

_____
_____
_____

B. Expanding Your Skill

Talk about the picture.

- What is happening in the picture?
- What has Rosa been doing?
- How many fish has she caught?
- What is the weather like? How can you tell?
- How do you think Rosa feels?

C. Exploring Language

Fishing is a water sport. Some sports need snow. Put each sport under the right heading on your paper.

swimming   skiing   sledding   diving   sailing

Water Sports	Snow Sports
_____	_____
_____	_____
_____	_____

After you have listed the sports, finish the following sentences.

My favorite sport is ____ .
When I play this sport, I feel ____ .
I can tell when others feel this way
because ____ .

D. Expressing Yourself

Do one of these things.

1. With a friend, write a story. Pretend that you two are the stars of a special sports event.
2. Write a letter to your favorite athlete. Describe what you like very much about her or him.

Father got Tara a new toy train. He will give it to Tara after school. Tara likes playing with toy trains.

Which is probably true?

(A) **Tara will be happy.**

(B) **Father is going away.**

Jim was walking home after school. It began to rain. Mother saw Jim and stopped the car. Jim got into the car.

Which is probably true?

(A) **Jim wanted to walk in the rain.**

(B) **Jim didn't get very wet.**

Mother went to the store. Bob stayed home. He made a surprise for Mother. When Mother came home, she was happy. Mother likes to eat cake.

Which is probably true?

(A) Bob made a cake.

(B) It was Bob's birthday.

There was paper on fire. Mother saw the fire. She ran into her house to get water.

Which is probably true?

(A) Mother hid in the house.

(B) Mother put water on the fire.

Ann cut the grass. Then she put her toys away. Mother came home and was surprised. Mother said, "I must get something for Ann."

Which is probably true?

(A) **Ann is too little to help.**

(B) **Ann made Mother happy.**

It's Tom's birthday. Many children are in Tom's house. They are waiting for him to come home. Tom does not know the children are in his house.

Which is probably true?

(A) **Tom will not come home.**

(B) **Tom will be surprised.**

Julia read a book. She liked the book. Julia said, "I will give the book to Bob. Bob likes to laugh."

Which is probably true?

(A) **The book is funny.**

(B) **Bob can't read.**

One day after school Ashley made a toy airplane. She painted it red. The next day she made a toy boat. She painted the boat blue.

Which is probably true?

(A) Ashley does not like school.

(B) Ashley likes to make things.

Jim lives on a farm. Sometimes his horse does not come when he calls. Then Jim gets food for the horse. Soon the horse comes to Jim.

Which is probably true?

(A) **The horse likes to eat.**

(B) **Jim's horse is slow.**

A truck came to Tom's house. In the truck was a new wagon. It was a green and yellow wagon. Father said, "Tom will be happy when he comes home."

Which is probably true?

(A) **The wagon is for Tom.**

(B) **Mother is in the truck.**

"Mary, come to the table," called Father. "It's time to eat." Mary didn't come. Father went to find her. Mary was reading a book.

Which is probably true?

(A) **The food was not ready.**

(B) **Mary didn't hear Father.**

Ann and Bob went to see a show. But the show was not funny. Ann said, "Let's go home." Ann and Bob didn't see the end of the show.

Which is probably true?

(A) **Ann and Bob laughed at the show.**

(B) **Ann and Bob didn't like the show.**

A. Exercising Your Skill

Look at the picture. Tom's friends are waiting to surprise him. It is Tom's birthday. Read the lists. In each list two of the words belong. One word does not belong. Write the headings on your paper. Then write the words that belong under each heading.

How Tom's Friends Feel

angry

happy

excited

How Tom Will Feel

surprised

pleased

sad

B. Expanding Your Skill

Pick the words from the box that tell about things at a birthday party. Write them on your paper. Then add some things to your list.

games	presents	homework
cake	maps	party favors

C. Exploring Language

Tell about what might have happened at Tom's birthday party. Copy the story that follows on your paper. Use your own words to fill in the blanks.

Tom's Special Day

Tom's friends were waiting to ＿＿ him. Tom felt ＿＿ ! Then everyone played ＿＿ . Tom's mother brought in the ＿＿ . His friends sang ＿＿ . At last Tom opened his ＿＿ . What a special day for Tom!

D. Expressing Yourself

Do one of these things.

1. Draw a picture of your favorite things to do at a birthday party. Have your classmates tell about what their favorite things are, too.

2. Write a thank you note from Tom to his friends. Tell about his feelings about the party.

3. In a small group, pretend you are Tom and his friends at the party. What does Tom say and do? How do his friends act? Act out the story.